WHAT IS THE METAVERSE?

What is the Metaverse?

MARK HARDING

Bald and Bonkers Network Academy

ISBN: 979-8-8691-9659-0
EISBN: 979-8-8691-9660-6

Disclaimer

This book is intended for informational purposes only. While every effort has been made to ensure its completeness and accuracy, errors in typography or content may occur. Additionally, the information contained herein is current only up to the date of publication. Therefore, consider this book a helpful guide rather than an infallible source.

The aim of this book is educational. The author and publisher do not guarantee the completeness of the information provided and cannot be held responsible for any errors or omissions. Neither the author nor the publisher accepts liability for any loss or damage, directly or indirectly, caused by the use of this book.

This book is meant for educational purposes and should not be relied upon as a replacement for professional medical advice, diagnosis, or treatment. Always consult a qualified healthcare professional for personalized medical guidance.

Contents

Disclaimer   v

1   Introduction   1

2   Understanding the Metaverse   3

3   The Metaverse Today   9

4   Criticisms and Concerns   14

5   Emerging Technology   27

6   How the Metaverse Will Transform
    the Future   38

7   Enhance Personal Life   48

8   Personalize Work and Education   54

9   Investment   60

10 Conclusion   65

Chapter 1

Introduction

In recent years, there has been a surge in discussions surrounding the Metaverse, captivating the attention of tech companies, thought leaders, and business proprietors alike. This concept promises to redefine the landscape of the internet, igniting both excitement and apprehension within various circles. The recent rebranding of Facebook to 'Meta' and their declared commitment to spearheading the development of the Metaverse has intensified the discourse, making the term more ubiquitous than ever before.

Yet, amidst the fervor, the Metaverse remains shrouded in ambiguity. What exactly is it? Who holds ownership over it? What possibilities does it offer? These pressing inquiries echo loudly, particularly in light of recent developments.

Fortunately, this comprehensive guide aims to demystify the Metaverse. We'll navigate through its intricacies, addressing these fundamental questions while elucidating why the Metaverse warrants your attention. Our objective is to equip you with a clear understanding, cutting through the clutter of misinformation that often obscures the complexities of this emerging phenomenon.

So, delve into the pages ahead. By the journey's end, you'll find yourself not only enlightened but also wondering why the concept of the Metaverse ever seemed perplexing in the first place.

Chapter 2

Understanding the Metaverse

In recent years, the allure of immersing one-self in virtual worlds, whether in video games, expansive digital realms, or the vast expanse of the internet, has captivated the imagination of millions. From the cinematic portrayals in "Wreck-It-Ralph Breaks The Internet" to the dystopian vision of "Ready Player One," the concept of the Metaverse has permeated count-less works of fiction, painting a vivid picture of a digital frontier where reality and fantasy intertwine.

Imagine a boundless virtual universe where users transcend the role of mere controllers, seamlessly embodying their avatars and navigating digital landscapes with unprecedented freedom and fluidity. In this realm, interactions are not confined to screens and keyboards but extend to immersive experiences where users engage with one another and influence the real world through their digital actions.

Moreover, the Metaverse holds the promise of bridging the gap between the virtual and real worlds, blurring boundaries like never before. Picture futuristic scenarios depicted in science fiction, where individuals don goggles providing augmented reality overlays of their surroundings, offering instant access to information about people, places, and objects. The Metaverse could potentially bring such technology into reality, enhancing our digital and physical experiences in ways previously unimaginable.

While the concept of the Metaverse may initially seem daunting, delving into its intricacies reveals its profound significance. Let's embark on this journey together, starting with a clear understanding of what the Metaverse entails.

At its core, the Metaverse represents a vast network of interconnected virtual environments, transcending geographical boundaries and allowing individuals to create, explore, and interact regardless of physical distance. Analogous to massively multiplayer online (MMO) games like Final Fantasy or World of Warcraft, users converge on shared servers, embodying avatars that traverse digital realms, engaging in activities, events, and even shaping economic systems.

Imagine the Metaverse as an expansive virtual realm, akin to a colossal shopping mall, where users access diverse servers owned by various entities. Whether navigating Amazon's virtual domain to shop with simple gestures or interacting with other users in shared virtual spaces, the Metaverse offers boundless possibilities for exploration and collaboration.

Furthermore, the significance of avatars

within the Metaverse cannot be overstated. These digital personas serve as extensions of ourselves, representing our presence and identity within virtual realms. As technology advances, avatars become increasingly lifelike, capable of expressing emotions and reactions in response to gestures and interactions, enriching the immersive experience of the Metaverse.

A key aspect of the Metaverse is its concept of persistence, ensuring continuity and presence across virtual environments. Whether accessed via smartphones, PCs, tablets, or VR headsets, users and their avatars maintain a consistent presence and appearance throughout the Metaverse. Changes made to an avatar's appearance or possessions persist across all platforms, reinforcing the seamless integration of virtual and real-world experiences.

While the vision of the Metaverse holds promise, its realization hinges on technological advancements and accessibility. Companies like Meta (formerly Facebook) are spearheading efforts to develop the necessary infrastructure, offering platforms and devices tailored for Metaverse exploration. Accessing the Metaverse may involve creating user accounts, customizing avatars, and gaining entry to a vast array of virtual worlds, each offering unique opportunities for exploration and interaction.

Despite significant progress in virtual reality (VR) technology, achieving a fully immersive Metaverse remains an ongoing endeavor. Current VR capabilities represent merely the tip of the iceberg compared to the envisioned potential of the Metaverse. Companies like Meta are investing heavily in research and development, with timelines ranging from 5 to 15 years for realizing the Metaverse's full potential. The technological landscape continues to evolve, presenting exciting prospects for those intrigued by advancements in virtual realms.

As we gaze into the horizon of technological innovation, the journey towards realizing the Metaverse holds promise and intrigue. The convergence of virtual and real-world experiences heralds a new frontier in human interaction and exploration, one that warrants attention and anticipation from enthusiasts and scholars alike. With each step forward, the Metaverse draws closer to becoming a tangible reality, reshaping our understanding of connectivity, creativity, and the very essence of human experience. As we delve deeper into the intricacies of the Metaverse, we uncover layers of complexity and potential, inviting us to explore, innovate, and redefine the boundaries of our digital existence.

Chapter 3

The Metaverse Today

As we embark on the exhilarating journey of exploring the Metaverse, it's apt to begin by drawing parallels to a realm familiar to many of us: video games. Virtual reality (VR) gaming serves as a precursor, offering tantalizing glimpses into the immersive experiences that the Metaverse promises to deliver. Yet, beyond the realm of gaming, several other facets offer profound insights into what the future Metaverse might entail, ushering in an era of unprecedented digital connectivity and interaction.

Video Games:

Massively multiplayer online (MMO) games such as Fortnite, Final Fantasy, Roblox, and World of Warcraft serve as microcosms of the Metaverse's potential. These sprawling digital realms provide fertile ground for exploration, collaboration, and creativity. Within these virtual landscapes, players inhabit avatars, forging friendships, engaging in epic quests, attending virtual events, and participating in bustling economies fueled by in-game currencies.

Customization options further enrich the experience, empowering players to sculpt avatars that mirror their fantasies or express their unique personalities. Whether soaring through the skies as a mythical creature or navigating urban landscapes as a digital doppelgänger, players revel in the freedom to shape their virtual identities.

Moreover, large-scale events and gatherings within MMOs foster a sense of community and camaraderie, echoing the inclusive and collaborative spirit envisioned for the Metaverse.

These digital rendezvous points serve as hubs for social interaction, cultural exchange, and shared experiences, laying the groundwork for the immersive social fabric of the Metaverse.

Virtual Reality (VR):

Virtual reality gaming represents a quantum leap in immersive entertainment, transcending the boundaries of conventional gaming experiences. By donning VR headsets, users are transported to alternate realities where they inhabit characters and interact with digital environments in unprecedented ways. Every action, from wielding a sword to traversing treacherous landscapes, is imbued with physicality, blurring the lines between the real and virtual worlds.

In its nascent stages, VR epitomizes the essence of the Metaverse, offering tantalizing glimpses into a future where digital landscapes seamlessly merge with physical reality. While current VR experiences primarily revolve around single-game environments, the Metaverse promises boundless exploration across interconnected virtual realms, each teeming with possibilities for adventure, social interaction, and creative expression.

Cryptocurrency:

In the realm of MMOs and virtual economies, transactions often revolve around virtual currencies tailored to specific game worlds. Similarly, the Metaverse is poised to embrace cryptocurrency as a primary medium of exchange, revolutionizing the way commerce is conducted within digital ecosystems. While traditional currencies retain their relevance, cryptocurrencies offer a decentralized, borderless alternative ideally suited for the fluid dynamics of the Metaverse.

Cryptocurrencies like Bitcoin serve as conduits between the physical and digital realms, facilitating seamless transactions within the Metaverse's sprawling ecosystem. As businesses and content creators increasingly integrate into virtual spaces, cryptocurrencies are set to proliferate, offering a frictionless means of conducting transactions and fostering economic activity within digital realms.

In anticipation of the Metaverse's emergence, familiarity with cryptocurrency becomes paramount. Despite its abstract nature, cryptocurrencies are gaining widespread acceptance as legitimate forms of payment, with an expanding network of vendors and service providers embracing digital currencies. In the Metaverse, the adoption of cryptocurrencies is poised to skyrocket, reshaping the landscape of virtual commerce and finance.

In essence, video games, virtual reality, and cryptocurrency serve as harbingers of the multifaceted landscape awaiting exploration within the Metaverse. As technological advancements continue to push the boundaries of digital innovation, these elements converge, paving the way for a virtual realm where reality and imagination intertwine, and boundless opportunities beckon to those daring enough to explore its depths.

Chapter 4

Criticisms and Concerns

In the ever-evolving landscape of technological advancement, the emergence of the Metaverse has sparked both intrigue and apprehension among the masses. While the concept of a virtual universe intertwining with our reality is still in its infancy, the critiques and uncertainties surrounding it are anything but new. As the Metaverse continues to develop, these concerns are poised to intensify, prompting a deeper examination of its implications for society and individuals alike.

Privacy Concerns:

At the forefront of apprehensions surrounding the Metaverse is the issue of privacy. With data breaches and privacy infringements commonplace in the digital sphere, questions abound regarding the security of personal information within the Metaverse. As users immerse themselves in this virtual realm, their actions, interactions, and even physical attributes may be scrutinized, raising concerns about data protection and potential leaks.

The necessity of webcams and sensors to create lifelike avatars further compounds these worries, as users must relinquish a significant amount of personal data to achieve virtual representation. As individuals engage in activities ranging from shopping to socializing within the Metaverse, the question of who has access to this data and how securely it is stored becomes paramount.

Addiction Risks:

The allure of screens and the dopamine-fueled feedback loops they provide present a significant concern within the Metaverse. As users immerse themselves in this virtual realm, the lines between reality and fantasy blur, potentially exacerbating issues of internet addiction. Unlike traditional browsing experiences where users can disconnect at will, the immersive nature of the Metaverse may make it increasingly difficult for individuals to disengage, leading to heightened dependency and psychological strain.

The prospect of escaping into a virtual world that offers excitement and stimulation surpassing reality poses a real threat to mental health, particularly for those susceptible to addictive behaviors. The Metaverse's potential to captivate users and provide an alternative to real-world challenges raises questions about the balance between virtual engagement and real-world responsibilities.

User Safety and Community Conduct:
Navigating the digital landscape comes with

its own set of challenges, including issues of cyberbullying, harassment, and online toxicity. While efforts are made to moderate online communities, the decentralized nature of the Metaverse poses unique challenges in maintaining a safe and inclusive environment for all users.

Instances of personal attacks and harassment within the Metaverse can have profound effects on individuals' well-being, as the virtual realm blurs the boundaries between online interactions and real-world consequences. The absence of effective safety measures and the decentralized governance structure raise concerns about accountability and the ability to address harmful behavior within this evolving digital ecosystem.

Social Implications:

The Metaverse holds the potential to serve as a platform for social activism and community engagement, offering avenues for like-minded individuals to connect and mobilize. However, it also poses risks of reinforcing echo chambers and facilitating the spread of harmful ideologies within segregated virtual spaces.

While the Metaverse may amplify voices of marginalized communities and facilitate global connectivity, it also raises questions about the propagation of misinformation and the proliferation of extremist views. Balancing the potential for positive social change with the risks of polarization and division remains a critical challenge as the Metaverse evolves.

Accessibility and Affordability:

The democratization of access to the Metaverse presents another significant hurdle, as the cost of entry may exclude marginalized communities and exacerbate existing disparities. While efforts are made to ensure affordability, the high price of VR technology and potential subscription fees may limit access to those with financial means.

Furthermore, the commercialization of the Metaverse raises questions about equity and ownership within this virtual realm. As companies vie for control and profit from virtual transactions, concerns arise about the commodification of digital experiences and the marginalization of those unable to afford entry.

As we contemplate the future of the Metaverse, it is essential to consider the profound impact it will have on society and individuals' lives. While the potential for innovation and connectivity is vast, addressing these complex challenges will be crucial in ensuring that the Metaverse remains a safe, inclusive, and equitable space for all. In the following sections, we will delve deeper into the technological advancements needed to realize the Metaverse's full potential and examine its implications for our evolving digital landscape.

Technological Advancements:

As the Metaverse continues to evolve, advancements in technology will play a pivotal role in shaping its development. From enhancing virtual reality experiences to bolstering security measures, ongoing innovation is essential to realizing the Metaverse's full potential.

Improved Virtual Reality (VR) Technology:

The immersive nature of the Metaverse hinges on the capabilities of VR technology. Continued advancements in VR hardware and software will be crucial in creating lifelike virtual environments and enhancing user experiences. From higher-resolution displays to more accurate motion tracking, the next generation of VR technology promises to blur the lines between the physical and digital worlds like never before.

Enhanced Security Protocols:

Addressing concerns surrounding privacy and data security will require robust security protocols tailored to the unique challenges of the Metaverse. Implementing encryption standards, data anonymization techniques, and decentralized authentication mechanisms will be essential in safeguarding user information and preventing unauthorized access. Additionally, incorporating AI-driven monitoring systems can help detect and mitigate potential threats in real-time, ensuring a safe and secure virtual environment for all users.

Blockchain Integration:

Blockchain technology holds promise as a means of enhancing transparency, decentralization, and trust within the Metaverse. By leveraging blockchain-based authentication and verification systems, users can maintain control over their digital identities and transactions, reducing reliance on centralized authorities. Smart contracts and decentralized autonomous organizations (DAOs) can also facilitate peer-to-peer transactions and governance mechanisms, fostering a more equitable and democratic virtual ecosystem.

Social and Ethical Considerations:

Beyond technological advancements, addressing social and ethical considerations will be essential in shaping the future of the Metaverse. From promoting digital literacy to fostering inclusivity and diversity, navigating the societal implications of virtual reality requires a multifaceted approach.

Promoting Digital Literacy:

As the Metaverse becomes increasingly integrated into everyday life, promoting digital literacy will be paramount in empowering users to navigate virtual environments responsibly. Providing educational resources and training programs on topics such as online safety, data privacy, and critical thinking can help users make informed decisions and mitigate potential risks within the Metaverse.

Fostering Inclusivity and Diversity:

Ensuring that the Metaverse is inclusive and representative of diverse voices and perspectives requires deliberate efforts to address issues of accessibility, representation, and discrimination. Implementing accessibility features for users with disabilities, promoting diverse avatar customization options, and establishing community guidelines that prohibit hate speech and discrimination are critical steps in fostering an inclusive virtual environment.

Ethical Design and Development:

Ethical considerations must guide the design and development of the Metaverse to prioritize user well-being and societal impact. Incorporating principles of human-centered design, ethical AI, and responsible data practices can help mitigate potential harms and promote positive social outcomes within the virtual realm. Additionally, fostering transparency and accountability in decision-making processes can engender trust and confidence among users, ensuring that the Metaverse serves the collective interests of society.

Regulatory and Governance Frameworks:

Navigating the regulatory landscape of the Metaverse will require collaboration between policymakers, industry stakeholders, and civil society to establish robust governance frameworks that balance innovation with accountability and user protection.

Regulatory Oversight:

Policymakers must work collaboratively with industry stakeholders to develop regulatory frameworks that address emerging challenges in the Metaverse while fostering innovation and competition. Key areas of focus may include data privacy, consumer protection, antitrust, and intellectual property rights, with an emphasis on promoting transparency, accountability, and user rights within virtual environments.

Industry Standards and Best Practices:

Establishing industry-wide standards and best practices will be essential in promoting interoper

ability, compatibility, and trust within the Metaverse ecosystem. Industry consortia, standards bodies, and collaborative initiatives can play a crucial role in developing and disseminating guidelines for responsible design, development, and operation of virtual platforms and services.

User Empowerment and Advocacy:

Empowering users to advocate for their rights and interests within the Metaverse is essential in ensuring that their voices are heard in regulatory and governance processes. Supporting grassroots organizations, consumer advocacy groups, and digital rights initiatives can amplify user concerns and priorities, influencing policy decisions and industry practices to align with user needs and preferences.

As we navigate the complex terrain of the

Metaverse's future, it's imperative to approach its development with a holistic understanding of its technological, social, and ethical dimensions. By fostering collaboration, innovation, and accountability, we can shape a Metaverse that reflects our collective values and aspirations, enriching the lives of users and communities worldwide.

Chapter 5

Emerging Technology

Accelerating Technological Trends Toward the Metaverse

In the ever-evolving landscape of technology, the trajectory toward the Metaverse is becoming increasingly tangible. While the complete realization of this virtual realm may still be on the horizon, the rapid pace of technological advancements is propelling us closer to its fruition. This chapter delves into the pivotal trends and innovations shaping the foundation of the Metaverse, from extended reality technologies to artificial intelligence and brain-computer interfaces.

Extended Reality Technologies:

Extended Reality (XR) technologies serve as the linchpin for bridging the gap between the physical and virtual worlds, laying the groundwork for the Metaverse's immersive experiences. Augmented Reality (AR), Virtual Reality (VR), and Mixed Reality (MR) collectively form the pillars of XR, each offering unique capabilities and applications.

Augmented Reality (AR):

Augmented Reality overlays digital content onto the real world, enriching our surroundings with virtual elements. From interactive filters on social media platforms to location-based gaming experiences like Pokémon Go, AR seamlessly integrates virtual and physical environments. Unlike VR, AR allows users to maintain awareness of their surroundings, fostering a blended reality that enhances rather than replaces the physical world.

Virtual Reality (VR):

Virtual Reality immerses users in fully digital environments, providing a 360-degree sensory experience. Whether for gaming, training simulations, or virtual meetings, VR transports users to alternate realities where they can interact with digital constructs. As VR technology continues to evolve, advancements in display resolution, motion tracking, and haptic feedback promise to elevate the realism and immersion of virtual experiences.

Mixed Reality (MR):

Mixed Reality merges digital and physical elements, enabling seamless interaction between the two realms. With MR headsets, users can place virtual objects in real-world environments and interact with them as if they were tangible objects. From virtual home design to immersive shopping experiences, MR blurs the boundaries between physical and digital spaces, offering unprecedented levels of interactivity and engagement.

Artificial Intelligence (AI):

Artificial Intelligence serves as the backbone of the Metaverse, powering everything from facial recognition to dynamic virtual interactions. As AI technology advances, it will play an increasingly integral role in shaping the user experience and driving innovation within virtual environments.

Facial Recognition and Avatar Realism:

AI-driven facial recognition software ensures that avatars accurately reflect users' appearances, enhancing realism and personalization within the Metaverse. By analyzing facial features and expressions, AI algorithms create lifelike representations of users in virtual environments, fostering a sense of identity and presence.

Dynamic NPCs and Intelligent Agents:

Artificial Intelligence enables the creation of dynamic Non-Player Characters (NPCs) and intelligent agents within the Metaverse. These

AI-driven entities populate virtual worlds, engaging with users in realistic and meaningful ways. Whether as virtual assistants, companions, or adversaries, NPCs powered by AI contribute to the richness and complexity of virtual environments.

Language Processing and Natural Interaction:

Advanced AI algorithms facilitate natural language processing and interaction within the Metaverse. By converting spoken or written language into machine-readable code, AI enables seamless communication between users and virtual entities. Whether engaging in realistic conversations or issuing voice commands, users can interact with virtual environments intuitively, enhancing immersion and user engagement.

Brain-Computer Interfaces (BCIs):

Brain-Computer Interfaces represent a paradigm shift in human-computer interaction, enabling direct communication between the brain and digital devices. While BCIs are still in early stages of development, they hold immense potential for revolutionizing the user experience within the Metaverse.

Neural Data Analysis and Interpretation:

BCIs analyze neural data to interpret users' intentions and commands, translating brain signals into actionable inputs within virtual environments. By bypassing traditional input devices, such as keyboards or controllers, BCIs offer a direct pathway for users to interact with virtual worlds, unlocking new levels of immersion and accessibility.

Surgical and Non-Invasive BCIs:

BCIs encompass a spectrum of technologies, ranging from non-invasive wearables to surgically implanted devices. While non-invasive BCIs offer accessibility and convenience, invasive implants provide unparalleled precision and fidelity. As research in neurotechnology advances, both surgical and non-invasive BCIs are poised to play pivotal roles in shaping the Metaverse's interface and user experience.

As we continue to harness the power of extended reality technologies, artificial intelligence, and brain-computer interfaces, the vision of the Metaverse edges closer to reality. With each technological leap, we inch closer to a future where virtual worlds intertwine seamlessly with our physical reality, reshaping how we work, play, and connect in the digital age.

Evolving Trends and Implications:

The convergence of these technological trends holds profound implications for the future of human-computer interaction and virtual experiences. As XR technologies mature and AI capabilities expand, the boundaries between the physical and virtual worlds blur, giving rise to a new era of immersive computing.

Social and Economic Paradigm Shifts:

The advent of the Metaverse heralds transformative shifts in social dynamics and economic structures. Virtual environments will serve as vibrant hubs for social interaction, commerce, and collaboration, transcending geographical barriers and fostering global communities. As individuals and businesses increasingly inhabit virtual spaces, traditional notions of identity, ownership, and value creation will undergo profound reevaluation.

Empowering Digital Economies:

The Metaverse promises to unleash a wave of innovation and entrepreneurship, fueling the growth of digital economies and decentralized ecosystems. From virtual real estate markets to virtual asset trading platforms, new economic models will emerge within virtual environments, offering opportunities for wealth creation and investment. As blockchain technology underpins digital asset ownership and transactions, the Metaverse will enable unprecedented levels of financial inclusion and empowerment.

Ethical and Regulatory Considerations:

Amidst the rapid evolution of XR technologies and AI-driven virtual experiences, ethical and regulatory considerations loom large. Privacy concerns surrounding data collection and surveillance in virtual environments demand robust safeguards and transparent governance frameworks. Additionally, ensuring equitable access to the Metaverse and addressing digital divides will be paramount to fostering inclusive and accessible virtual communities.

Cultural and Societal Impact:

The Metaverse's cultural impact extends beyond mere technological innovation, shaping narratives, identities, and collective experiences. From virtual art galleries to immersive cultural exhibitions, virtual environments will serve as canvases for creative expression and cultural exchange. However, as virtual spaces increasingly influence social norms and behaviors, critical dialogue surrounding digital citizenship, online safety, and digital well-being becomes imperative.

Educational Paradigm Shifts:

Virtual environments offer unparalleled opportunities for immersive and experiential learning, revolutionizing traditional educational paradigms. From virtual classrooms to interactive simulations, the Metaverse empowers learners to explore diverse subjects and environments, transcending the limitations of physical space and resources. As educators embrace virtual pedagogies, the Metaverse holds the potential to democratize access to quality education and foster lifelong learning.

Environmental Sustainability:

While the Metaverse presents boundless possibilities for digital exploration and interaction, it also raises concerns regarding environmental sustainability. The energy consumption associated with XR technologies and virtual infrastructures necessitates mindful consideration of eco-friendly practices and renewable energy solutions. As virtual worlds expand and scale, prioritizing sustainability and minimizing carbon footprints will be imperative to ensuring a sustainable Metaverse ecosystem.

Conclusion:

In conclusion, the trajectory toward the Metaverse represents a transformative journey at the nexus of technology, society, and human experience. As XR technologies, artificial intelligence, and brain-computer interfaces converge, the Metaverse emerges as a paradigm-shifting phenomenon with far-reaching implications for humanity. By navigating the opportunities and challenges inherent in this digital frontier, we embark on a collective exploration of the possibilities and potentials of virtual existence. As we venture further into the Metaverse, let us embrace innovation, foster inclusivity, and uphold ethical principles to shape a future where virtual and physical realities intertwine harmoniously.

Chapter 6

How the Metaverse Will Transform the Future

The impending integration of the metaverse into our lives promises a seismic shift in how we perceive and interact with the world around us. Although much about the metaverse remains shrouded in mystery, its potential to revolutionize various facets of our existence is undeniable. Let's delve deeper into the ways in which the metaverse will reshape our future.

Workplace Evolution:

One of the most significant impacts of the metaverse lies in its ability to revolutionize the workplace. By transcending geographical constraints, virtual environments facilitate seamless communication and collaboration among individuals scattered across the globe. Picture this: instead of cramming into a physical boardroom for a meeting, employees can convene in a virtual space, interacting as lifelike avatars. Remote work will no longer be an exception but the norm, with virtual job opportunities opening doors for freelancers and remote workers worldwide.

Remote Work Reinvented:

The metaverse heralds an era of unparalleled flexibility, with nearly every job offering a virtual option. No longer bound by physical office locations, professionals can work from anywhere, leveraging the power of virtual connectivity. Whether you're based in Georgia or working for a company in Canada, geographical barriers dissolve as the metaverse becomes your new workspace.

Healthcare and Defense Advancements:

In healthcare and defense, virtual reality (VR) technology is already making waves, transforming training and simulation experiences. Soldiers can undergo realistic combat training without risking physical harm, while surgeons hone their skills through immersive VR simulations. The metaverse amplifies these capabilities, enabling remote surgical procedures and immersive combat scenarios, all within a safe and controlled virtual environment.

Innovations in Product Development:

With its hyper-realistic simulations, the metaverse offers a sandbox for manufacturers and businesses to prototype and test new concepts. From automotive design to consumer electronics, virtual testing environments minimize risks associated with physical prototypes, accelerating innovation and reducing time-to-market. By validating designs within the metaverse, companies can optimize resources and streamline product development processes.

Personal Transformation:

On a personal level, the metaverse promises to redefine how we experience leisure and social interaction. Imagine traversing majestic mountains, swimming in serene lakes, or exploring bustling cities—all within the immersive confines of the metaverse. Beyond visual engagement, advancements in haptic technology and sensory feedback enhance the multisensory experience, allowing users to touch, smell, and taste their virtual surroundings.

Unleashing Creativity and Imagination:

In the metaverse, creativity knows no bounds. Users can embody fantastical avatars, from mythical creatures to sports icons, transcending the limitations of physical reality. Childhood fantasies of exploring jungles as a monkey or emulating sports heroes come to life in the virtual realm, fostering imagination and self-expression on an unprecedented scale.

Learning and Connection:

Moreover, the metaverse serves as a hub for learning and intellectual exchange. Whether reconnecting with long-lost friends or attending virtual lectures by esteemed scholars, the metaverse transcends physical barriers, fostering connections and knowledge-sharing across continents. From vast digital libraries to interactive educational experiences, the metaverse democratizes access to information and fosters lifelong learning.

Navigating the Metaverse:

As the metaverse becomes a tangible reality, navigating its vast landscapes requires strategic foresight and adaptability. Part III of this book will equip you with the tools and insights needed to harness the full potential of the metaverse. From optimizing your virtual presence to leveraging emerging technologies, discover how to navigate this transformative frontier and unlock new opportunities in your personal and professional life.

Unlocking the Metaverse: A Comprehensive Guide

As the metaverse inches closer to becoming a tangible reality, it's essential to prepare for its integration into our lives. In this section, we'll explore the practicalities of using the metaverse and uncover the myriad opportunities it presents for personal growth and advancement.

Embracing Digital Transformation:

As with any technological advancement, embracing the metaverse requires a willingness to adapt and evolve. From investing in the necessary hardware to familiarizing oneself with virtual platforms and interfaces, navigating the metaverse demands a proactive approach to digital literacy. Whether you're a seasoned tech enthusiast or a novice explorer, embracing the metaverse opens doors to a world of possibilities.

Creating Your Virtual Identity:

Central to the metaverse experience is the concept of digital identity. As you step into the virtual realm, you'll have the opportunity to craft a persona that reflects your aspirations and preferences. From selecting your avatar's appearance to curating your virtual environment, the metaverse offers unprecedented freedom in self-expression. Embrace this opportunity to redefine yourself and explore new facets of your identity in the digital realm.

Exploring Virtual Realms:

Navigating the vast landscapes of the metaverse requires a spirit of adventure and exploration. From bustling virtual cities to serene natural landscapes, the metaverse is teeming with immersive environments waiting to be discovered. Whether you're seeking thrills in virtual theme parks or tranquility in virtual retreats, the metaverse offers endless opportunities for exploration and discovery.

Connecting with Others:

At the heart of the metaverse lies the power of connection. As you traverse its digital landscapes, you'll encounter a diverse array of individuals from around the globe. Embrace the opportunity to forge meaningful relationships, collaborate on projects, and engage in lively discussions with like-minded individuals. Whether you're attending virtual meetups, participating in shared experiences, or simply striking up conversations with fellow explorers, the metaverse fosters a sense of community and camaraderie unlike any other.

Leveraging Virtual Tools:

In the metaverse, tools and utilities abound, offering practical solutions to everyday challenges. From virtual productivity suites to immersive learning platforms, the metaverse empowers users to work, learn, and play more efficiently than ever before. Explore the myriad virtual tools available and discover how they can enhance your personal and professional endeavors.

Ensuring Privacy and Security:

Amidst the excitement of exploring the metaverse, it's crucial to prioritize privacy and security. As you interact with others and share personal information within virtual environments, take proactive measures to safeguard your digital identity and data. Familiarize yourself with privacy settings, encryption protocols, and cybersecurity best practices to mitigate risks and protect your online presence.

Embracing the Future:

As we stand on the brink of the metaverse's emergence, it's essential to approach this new frontier with a sense of optimism and curiosity. Embrace the transformative potential of the metaverse and seize the opportunity to shape its evolution. By embracing digital innovation, fostering meaningful connections, and leveraging virtual resources, you'll unlock new horizons of possibility within the metaverse and embark on a journey of endless discovery and growth.

Chapter 7

Enhance Personal Life

The Metaverse: A Paradigm Shift in Human Experience

The internet revolutionized the way we live, work, and connect with others. From facilitating new career opportunities to fostering global friendships, its impact on society has been profound. Yet, as we stand on the cusp of a new era with the impending arrival of the metaverse, we find ourselves on the brink of an even greater transformation. The metaverse promises to amplify the benefits of the internet exponentially, offering unprecedented levels of immersion, connectivity, and possibility.

Gaming: A Gateway to Virtual Realms

Central to the allure of the metaverse is its potential to revolutionize gaming. While MMO games and VR technology have provided glimpses into what the metaverse may entail, the true extent of its capabilities remains untapped. Drawing inspiration from sci-fi masterpieces like "Ready Player One," the metaverse promises a convergence of virtual worlds, where players can seamlessly interact, compete, and collaborate on an unprecedented scale.

In the metaverse, gaming transcends mere entertainment to become a fully immersive second life. From the visceral sensation of battle to the thrill of exploration, every aspect of the gaming experience is heightened by the immersive power of the metaverse. Players will not merely observe the virtual world but inhabit it fully, engaging their senses in ways previously unimaginable.

Beyond traditional gaming, the metaverse opens up new frontiers for interactive experiences, from immersive storytelling to collaborative problem-solving. Virtual worlds become playgrounds for creativity and exploration, where users can shape their own destinies and forge lasting connections with others.

Social Dynamics: Redefining Connection

Beyond gaming, the metaverse offers boundless opportunities for social interaction and connection. Unlike traditional social media platforms, where interactions remain largely confined to screens, the metaverse enables users to engage in shared experiences in virtual space. Whether it's attending virtual concerts, exploring virtual landscapes, or simply hanging out with friends in digital environments, the metaverse redefines the boundaries of social interaction.

Dating, too, takes on a new dimension in the metaverse, where individuals can forge meaningful connections in immersive virtual environments. Gone are the days of awkward first dates and superficial interactions; in the metaverse, users can truly get to know each other on a deeper level, unencumbered by the constraints of physical distance.

Moreover, the metaverse offers a platform for self-expression and creativity, allowing users to share their passions and talents with a global audience. Whether it's hosting virtual events, teaching virtual classes, or showcasing artistic creations, the metaverse provides a fertile ground for innovation and collaboration.

Escapism and Wellness: Finding Solace in Virtual Realms

In an increasingly hectic world, the metaverse offers a sanctuary for relaxation and rejuvenation. Whether seeking solace on a virtual beach, retreating to a cozy cabin in the woods, or enjoying quality time with loved ones by a virtual fireplace, users can escape the stresses of everyday life and immerse themselves in tranquil digital environments.

Yet, to fully unlock the potential of the

metaverse, users must invest in the necessary technology. Haptic suits, immersive headsets, robust internet connections, and accounts across various metaverse platforms are essential tools for navigating this new frontier. While the initial investment may seem daunting, the rewards of immersive virtual experiences are boundless, offering a glimpse into a future where the boundaries between the physical and digital worlds blur indefinitely.

Embracing the Future: Charting a Course for Metaverse Adoption

As we stand on the threshold of this new era, it's essential to embrace the opportunities that the metaverse presents while also addressing the challenges it may bring. Education and outreach will play a crucial role in ensuring widespread adoption and understanding of metaverse technologies, empowering individuals to leverage its potential for personal and professional growth.

Moreover, collaboration between industry

stakeholders, policymakers, and technologists will be essential in shaping a metaverse that is inclusive, accessible, and beneficial for all. By working together to address concerns such as privacy, security, and digital equity, we can create a metaverse that enriches lives and enhances human connection on a global scale.

In conclusion, the metaverse represents a paradigm shift in human experience, offering unparalleled opportunities for exploration, connection, and self-expression. By embracing this transformative technology and charting a course for responsible adoption, we can unlock the full potential of the metaverse and usher in a new era of human possibility.

Chapter 8

Personalize Work and Education

Unlocking the Potential of the Metaverse for Education and Work

In the boundless expanse of the metaverse, where virtual realms await exploration, there lies a transformative force that extends far beyond mere entertainment. It's a force poised to revolutionize the very foundations of education and work, ushering in an era of unprecedented opportunity and innovation. As we embark on this journey into the digital frontier, let us delve deeper into the myriad ways in which the metaverse will shape the future of learning and productivity.

Virtual Workspaces: Redefining the Concept of Work

Picture a world where the traditional boundaries of the office fade away, replaced by virtual workspaces that transcend physical limitations. No longer constrained by geographic location or commuting constraints, individuals from all corners of the globe converge in virtual realms to collaborate, communicate, and create. Gone are the days of rigid nine-to-five schedules and monotonous office routines; instead, flexibility becomes the hallmark of the modern workplace.

With the metaverse as our gateway, professionals gain unprecedented freedom to shape their work environment to suit their needs. Whether it's conducting meetings in immersive virtual boardrooms or collaborating on projects in virtual offices, the possibilities are as limitless as the digital horizon. Moreover, the metaverse fosters a sense of connection and community among remote teams, bridging the gap between physical distances and fostering collaboration on a global scale.

But the benefits of virtual workspaces extend far beyond convenience; they also have profound implications for productivity and efficiency. By eliminating the distractions and inefficiencies associated with traditional office settings, virtual workspaces empower individuals to focus on their tasks and achieve greater levels of productivity. With the metaverse as our workplace, the only limit to what we can achieve is our imagination.

Online Curriculums and Virtual Classrooms: A Revolution in Education

In the metaverse, education transcends the confines of physical classrooms and traditional curriculums, offering a dynamic and immersive learning experience. Here, learners have the opportunity to explore a vast array of subjects and disciplines, guided by educators and experts

from around the world. From interactive lectures to hands-on simulations, the metaverse
transforms education into an engaging and personalized journey of discovery.

Gone are the days of one-size-fits-all curriculums and rigid learning structures; in the
metaverse, learners have the freedom to chart
their own educational path. Whether it's mas-
tering a new skill, exploring a passion project,
or delving into cutting-edge research, the metaverse provides a platform for lifelong learning
and personal growth. Moreover, the interactive
nature of virtual classrooms fosters collaboration, critical thinking, and creativity, preparing
learners for success in an increasingly digital
world.

But perhaps the most exciting aspect of
education in the metaverse is its potential to
transcend the boundaries of time and space.
Through immersive simulations and virtual experiences, students can journey to distant
lands, explore historical events, and engage
with complex concepts in ways never before

possible. This active learning approach not only enhances retention but also fosters a deeper understanding of the subject matter.

As we look to the future, the metaverse holds the promise of democratizing education and expanding access to learning opportunities for all. By harnessing the power of technology and embracing the transformative potential of the metaverse, we can unlock new pathways to knowledge and empower individuals to thrive in an ever-changing world.

Embracing the Future: Navigating the Digital Frontier

In conclusion, the metaverse represents a paradigm shift in how we approach education and work, offering boundless opportunities for innovation, collaboration, and personal growth. As we venture forth into this brave new world, let us embrace the possibilities that await and seize the opportunity to shape the future of learning and productivity. Together, we can harness the power of the metaverse to create

a brighter, more inclusive, and more interconnected world for generations to come.

Chapter 9

Investment

The advent of the metaverse promises not only to revolutionize digital entertainment but also to reshape the very fabric of our economy, education, and social interactions. As explored in previous chapters, the metaverse is poised to become a thriving ecosystem with its own unique economy, akin to the intricate virtual economies found within video games. This digital landscape will be intricately linked to cryptocurrency, offering investors a myriad of opportunities to capitalize on its growth potential while the metaverse is still in its infancy.

Metaverse Stocks: A Window into the Future

Investing in companies poised to lead the charge in metaverse innovation offers investors a front-row seat to the digital transformation unfolding before our eyes. Companies like NIKE, which have already established a presence in virtual realms like Nikeland within ROBLOX, exemplify the potential for merging real-world brands with virtual experiences. With NIKE's strategic focus on dominating the market for virtual apparel and accessories, investing in such companies provides investors with exposure to the burgeoning metaverse economy.

Furthermore, technology companies are positioned at the forefront of metaverse development, driving innovation in areas such as cloud computing, virtual reality, and artificial intelligence. Amazon, Microsoft, and other tech giants are not only shaping the infrastructure of the metaverse but also stand to reap substantial rewards as the demand for virtual solutions continues to soar. Investing in these companies offers investors a stake in the very foundation

of the metaverse, with the potential for significant long-term growth.

NFT Investments: Unlocking the Power of Digital Ownership

Non-Fungible Tokens (NFTs) have emerged as a cornerstone of the metaverse economy, offering a novel approach to digital ownership and authenticity. As the backbone of virtual asset ownership, NFTs enable investors to acquire unique digital assets, ranging from digital collectibles to virtual real estate. By leveraging blockchain technology, NFTs provide immutable proof of ownership, empowering investors to assert control over their digital assets across various platforms and experiences.

The versatility of NFTs extends beyond mere ownership, offering avenues for creators and investors to monetize their digital creations. From artwork and music to virtual experiences and in-game assets, NFTs represent a new frontier in the digital economy, with the potential to unlock untapped value for investors. As the metaverse continues to evolve, investing in NFTs provides investors with a unique opportunity to participate in the digital asset revolution and capitalize on emerging trends.

Virtual Estates: Building the Foundations of the Metaverse

Virtual real estate has emerged as a focal point of investment within the metaverse, offering investors the opportunity to acquire prime parcels of digital land in anticipation of future growth. Platforms like Decentraland, The Sandbox, Crypto Voxels, and Somnium Space provide fertile ground for investors to stake their claim in the virtual landscape. By acquiring virtual estates, investors gain access to a blank canvas for creativity, commerce, and community-building.

The potential applications of virtual real estate are vast, ranging from hosting virtual events and exhibitions to establishing virtual businesses and entertainment venues. As the metaverse expands, virtual estates will become increasingly valuable assets, serving as hubs for social interaction, economic activity, and creative expression. By investing in virtual estates, investors position themselves at the forefront of this digital frontier, with the potential to reap substantial rewards as the metaverse continues to evolve.

Conclusion: Embracing the Future of Investment

As we stand on the cusp of a new era in digital innovation, the metaverse offers a wealth of opportunities for investors seeking to capitalize on emerging trends. Whether through metaverse stocks, NFT investments, or virtual estates, the avenues for investment are as diverse as they are promising. By embracing the transformative power of the metaverse and seizing the opportunities it presents, investors can position themselves for success in the digital economy of tomorrow.

Chapter 10

Conclusion

The Metaverse stands as a captivating and occasionally perplexing realm on the horizon, poised to reshape our existence in profound ways. Through the pages of this book, our aim has been to demystify the notion of the Metaverse, offering clarity and insight into its potential impact on our lives. While immediate investment or preparation for its advent may not be at the forefront of your mind, understanding the boundless opportunities it presents is crucial.

Despite the fact that the full realization

of the Metaverse may still be several decades away, its inevitability is palpable, driven by the relentless march of technological progress. Already, we are witnessing glimpses of its emergence through the proliferation of VR systems and the integration of advanced technologies into various facets of our daily routines.

Indeed, the prospect of the Metaverse is nothing short of captivating, promising to revolutionize our work, education, social interactions, and modes of self-expression. Its arrival heralds a seismic shift in the fabric of our society, offering a new frontier where the boundaries between the physical and digital worlds blur into obscurity.

Whether you envision yourself as an enthusiastic participant in the immersive experiences the Metaverse has to offer, a diligent contributor shaping its development, or a savvy investor capitalizing on its potential, this book aims to equip you with the knowledge and insights needed to navigate this brave new world.

Yet, as we eagerly anticipate the arrival of the Metaverse, we must also acknowledge the patience required as we await its full realization. For while the journey may be lengthy, the destination promises to be nothing short of extraordinary, offering boundless opportunities for exploration, innovation, and growth.